God's Word for Me

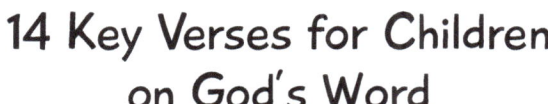

14 Key Verses for Children on God's Word

BIBLE CHAPTERS FOR KIDS

God is pleased when I obey His words and spend time with Him in prayer.

"Blessed are those who keep His testimonies, and that seek Him with their whole heart."

(verse 2)

I read and treasure God's Word. When I study it, I can learn about doing what is right.

"Your Word have I hid in mine heart, that I might not sin against You."
(verse 11)

When I read God's Word,
I take time to think about
it, so I can be sure of
what do to.

"I will meditate
in Your precepts,
and respect
Your ways."

(verse 15)

I enjoy reading God's Word and I do my best to live it every day.

"I will delight myself in Your statutes: I will not forget Your Word."
(verse 16)

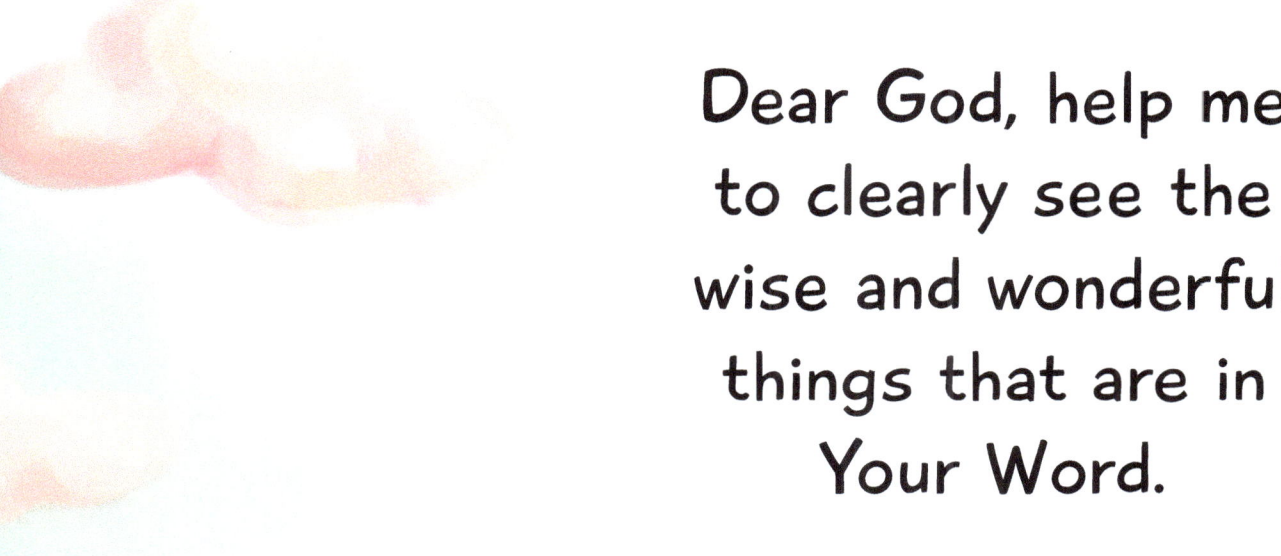

Dear God, help me to clearly see the wise and wonderful things that are in Your Word.

"Open my eyes, that I may behold wondrous things out of Your law."

(verse 18)

God's word is full of good advice, which fills me with joy and happiness.

"Your Testimonies are my delight and my counselors."
(verse 24)

Dear God, help me to understand what I read in your word, so that I can do my best to follow it.

"Give me understanding, and I will keep your law; I will observe it with my whole heart."

(verse 34)

God's Word helps me to think more about others, rather than about my own desires.

"Incline my heart unto Thy testimonies, and not to covetousness."

(verse 36)

When I disobey, things don't work out well for me. I have learned from my mistakes and now I follow Your Word.

"Before I was afflicted I went astray: but now have I kept Your Word."

(verse 67)

God is eternal, and so is His Word. I can depend on it forever.

"Forever, oh Lord, Your Word is settled in heaven."
(verse 89)

I love to read God's Word. I think about it a lot as I go through my day.

"Oh how I love Your law! It is my meditation all the day."
(verse 97)

God's Word is a sweet comfort to me. It can be even more pleasurable than tasty sweets!

"How sweet are Your words to my taste. Yea, sweeter than honey to my mouth."
(verse 103)

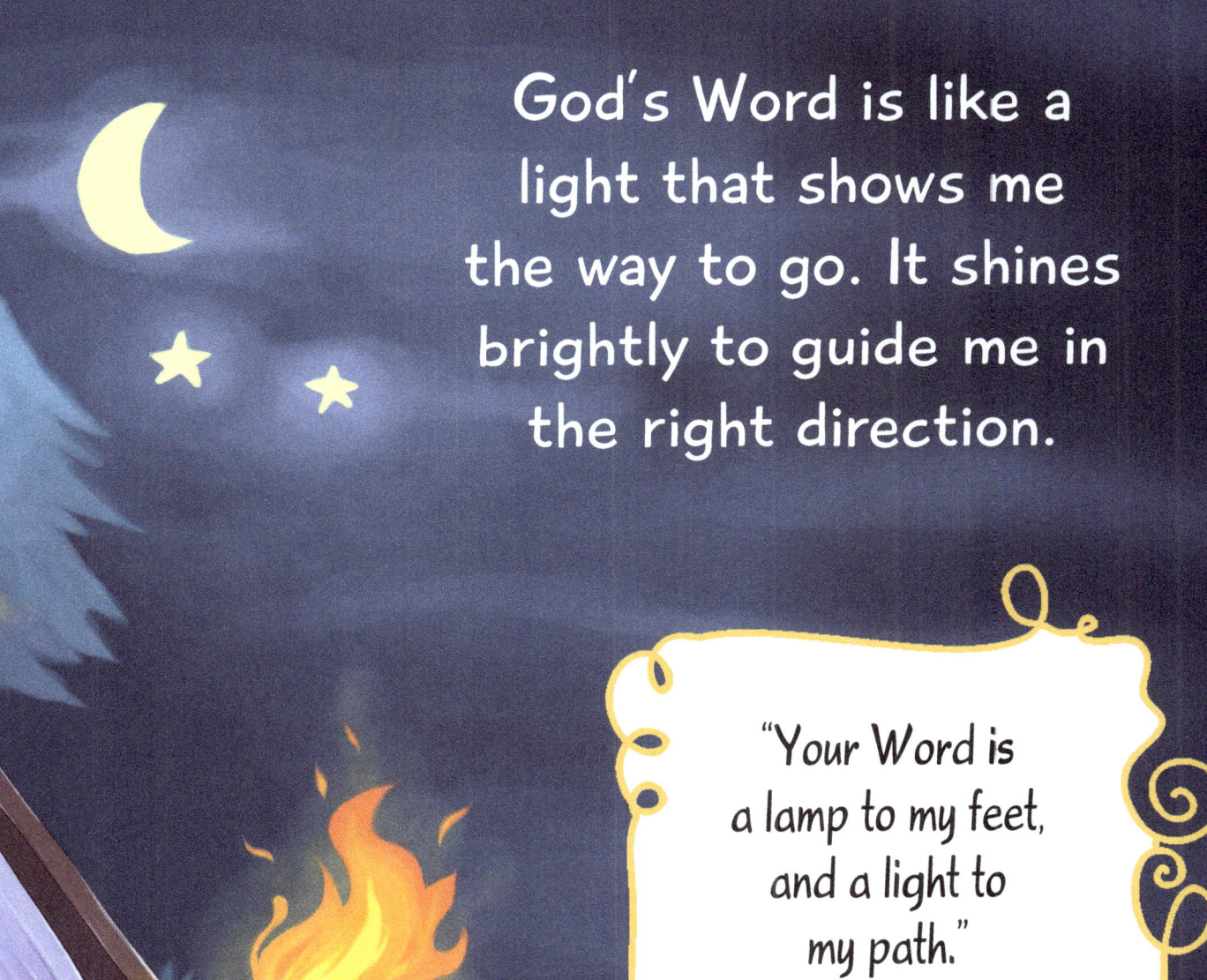

God's Word is like a light that shows me the way to go. It shines brightly to guide me in the right direction.

"Your Word is a lamp to my feet, and a light to my path."

(verse 105)

When I spend a lot of time reading God's Word, I feel at peace and nothing can trouble me.

"Great peace have they which love Your law: and nothing will offend them."

(verse 165)

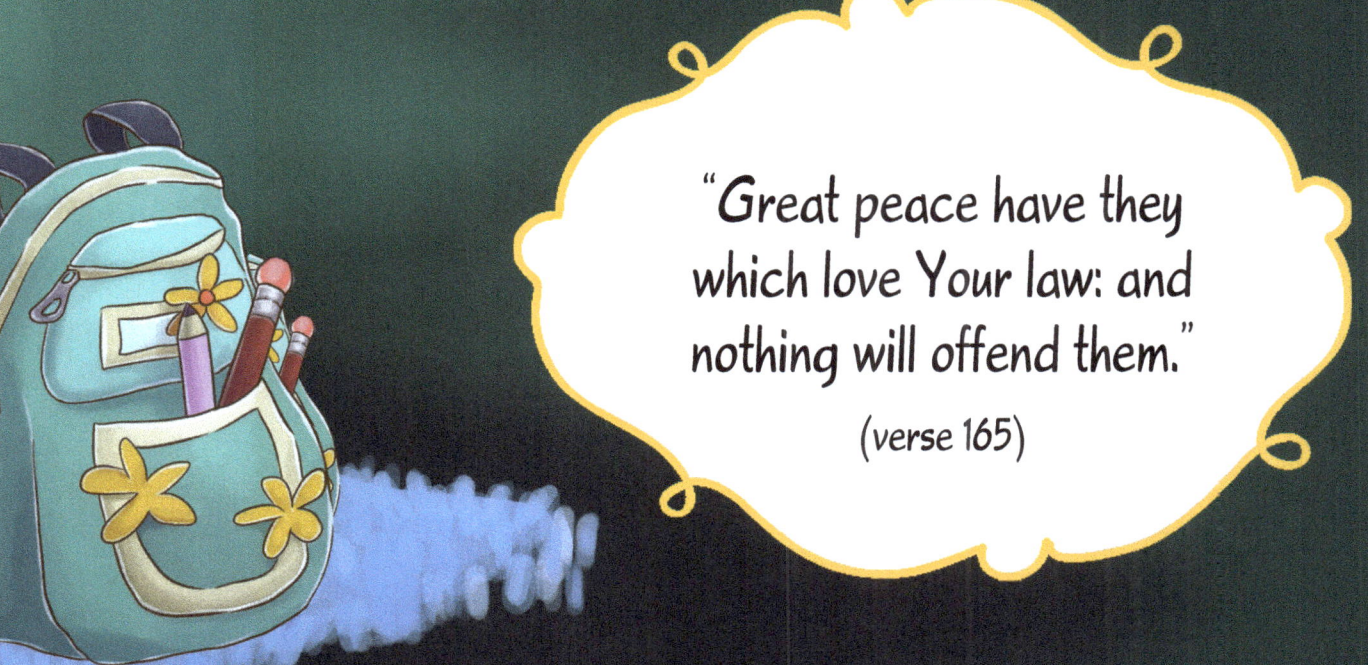

Fun Facts

Check out some of the **different** names for **God's Word** in this chapter of the Bible.

More books in the series:

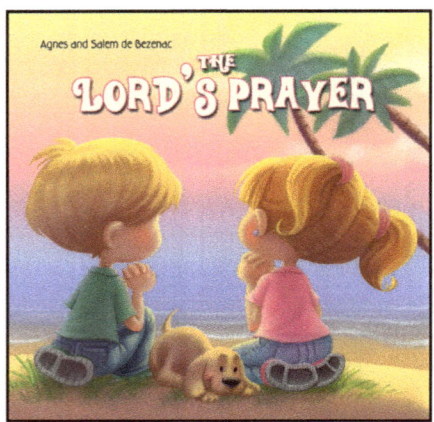
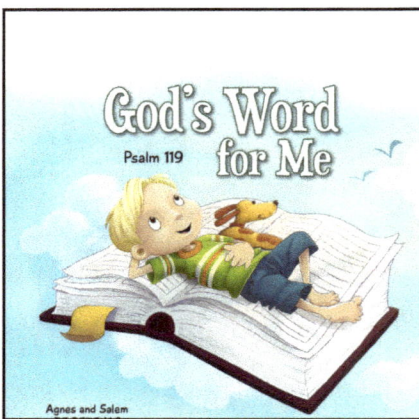

iCHARACTER

Published by iCharacter Ltd. (Ireland)
www.iCharacter.org
By Agnes and Salem de Bezenac
Illustrated by Agnes de Bezenac
Colored by Fiona P and Henny Y.
Copyright. All rights reserved.
All Bible verses adapted from the KJV.

Copyright © 2014 iCharacter Limited. All rights reserved. No part of this book may be reproduced in any form or by any electronic or mechanical means, including information storage and retrieval systems, without written permission from the publisher or author, except in the case of a reviewer, who may quote brief passages embodied in critical articles or in a review.